ISBN: 9978-9901-6-X
Copyright: JORGE ANHALZER
Design: AZUCA
Printing: IMPRENTA MARISCAL
Translation into English: CAMILO ANDRADE
Scientific supervision: DR. JAVIER SILVA

Identification of species:
General zoology: JUAN CARLOS MATEUS
Botany: CARMEN JOSSE
Ornithology: JUAN MANUEL CARRION
Mammalogy: JUAN J. ESPINOSA
Entomology: DIEGO BASTIDAS
Herpetology: JEAN MARC TOUZET
Map: HUGO IDROVO
Field asistant: ROMULO CARDENAS

The National Parks and protected areas of Ecuador are
controlled by the forestry department of the Ministerio de
Agricultura y Ganadería. I would like to express my
gratitude to all employees of the above mentioned depar-
tament including the Park guards and administrative staff
who are contributing in such a manner maintain this
world heritage in benefit of mankind.

NATIONAL PARKS OF ECUADOR

ECUADOR

Photography and text by Jorge Juan Anhalzer

In defiance of its small size, Ecuador is a land of remarkable beauty and diverse climates, with a folk and history which are closely related. The natural sanctuaries and their varied forms of life, are unique and dissimilar.

Let us envision an imaginary trip into the past. We start our journey somewhere in the middle of the Pacific ocean, heading eastwards in the direction of the rising sun. The Galápagos islands appear ahead as an exotic paradise isolated by hundreds of miles from the rest of the world. They give us the impression of our having blundered back millennia through time. Thus we visualize the idyllic relationship between the living creatures and their surrounding environment which represents the basis of survival and perpetuation of life on earth. We resume our trip, still heading due east, reaching the continent much before the spanish conquest took place.

From our imagination-borne vehicle we observe vast jungles covering the pristine land with their superb greenery. They extend yearningly, trying to reach the crystalline waters of the sea. Unlike in the Galápagos, we notice the presence of other animals and plants, but especially, human beings appear to be ubiquitous in all places. These primeval peoples seem to maintain a harmonious peace and concord with their natural environment. In their lives around the villages and tilled lands, there is nothing that may conceal the fact of this amazing harmony.

Proceeding with our trip, we leave behind the ocean in order to explore the lush forests of the lowlands. We observe innumerable meandering rivers running in opposite directions, suddenly, the huge green savannah gives way to tortured, serrated ranks which vanish abruptly into the clouds. After tantalizing moments we emerge in a lofty world scattered with huge snow-capped mountains and smoking volcanoes.

In the valleys we find large concentrations of peoples whose main consuetudinary task seems to be that of waging wars. These aborigines demonstrate a deeply engrained attitude of concern and respect for the earth which they call in Quichua " Pacha mama " or mother earth, since it has given them life and the same unalterable destiny will be bestowed upon future generations.

Having left behind us the peoples from the hills, we explore new territories. As we head east, the precipitous gorges of the mountains become less and less dramatic and extensive jungles and huge rivers come into view. Since our means of conveyance is noiseless, we can clearly hear the twitter of the birds, whose voices gladden the countryside. The shrilling cries of monkeys pervades the scene, yet the quiet flow of rivers creates an atmosphere of overwhelming serenity.

As this marvelous trip ends, we return to the present day. We travel through time and unexpectedly land in an unknown country called Ecuador. To our consternation, we observe an alarming scene; thousands of people

PODOCARPUS P.

FERNANDINA I.

ISABELA

BARTHO
SANTIAG
JAMES I.

MARC

FLOREANA I.

BALTRA I.
STA. CRUZ I.
STA. FE I.

ESPAÑOLA I.
HOOD I.

GALAP

SAN CRISTOBAL I.
CHATHAM L.

resembling ant colonies proceeding to raze the green wilderness, thus leaving treeless, dull spots in all directions. The rivers become continually darker due to the erosive action of water upon unprotected land, concrete buildings fill the landscape. Filthy garbage appears scattered everywhere. This is the law of absurdity in the present days, it manifests itself most horribly in its destructive effect on nature caused by our societies whose complicated conditions of life can only be calculated with great subtlety and difficulty.

At the end of this trip, we must draw our own conclusions by asking the question: what would have happened if we had continued the journey into the future?

Fortunately, several preserved areas, remain in their natural state, and thus provide a taste of what all Ecuador once was. These National Parks not only represent a scenic beauty, but also enlighten us as to the great value of undisturbed wilderness.

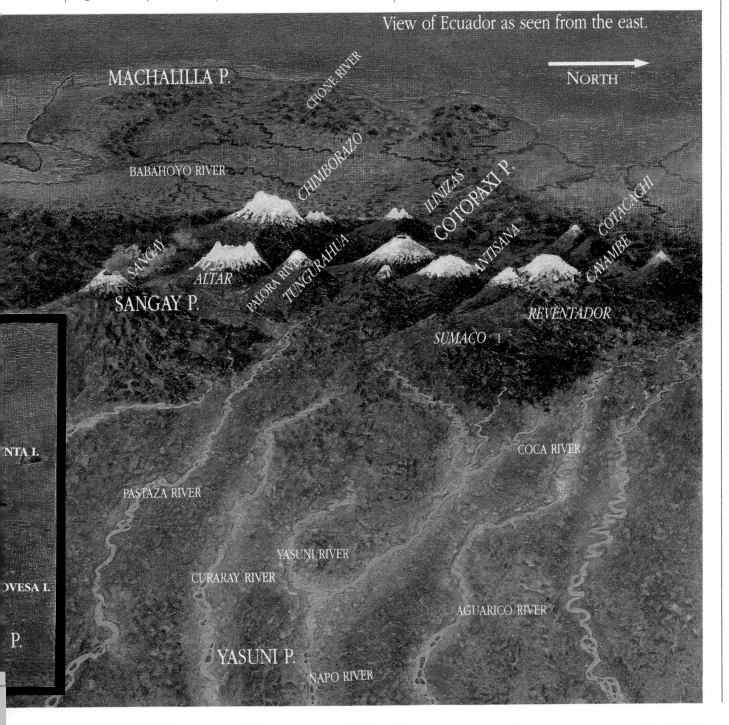

View of Ecuador as seen from the east.

NATIONAL PARK

COTOPAXI

In the 17th century when the measurements of the earth were made by the French geodesical expedition, it was realized that the globe was rather flattened at the poles. This fact ascertained that Chimborazo was the highest mountain on earth if measured from the center of it, consequently Cotopaxi occupies the second or maybe the third place, considering that Cayambe, though lower, lies much closer to the equator. Despite their proximity to the sun, all these places are utterly desolate due to the altitude and perennial cold. It is in fact the energy of the sun that makes the sub-atomic particles in the atmosphere to collide producing heat, but in the heights the air is so thin that the atomic particles are much separated from each other, therefore having less chance to collide releasing but little heat.

Insects, reptiles and amphibians cannot regulate their body temperature, for they take it from the environment, therefore they are known as "cold-blooded" creatures though in some occasions their blood can be warmer than mammals. Hence these animals rarely adapt themselves to the heights since the majority of them perish when the temperature approaches the freezing point, because their nervous membranes lose their pliability and semi-liquid condition which are necessary to transmit electric signals.

A small species of frog, the so-called "Jambato" is one of the few exceptions of cold-blooded animals that lives in these heights. The Jambato is dressed in a dark colour in order to take advantage of the sun rays and has strictly diurnal habits. It usually dwells near lakes or ponds because the air in the moorlands is extremely dry.

Mammals and birds are far better fit to survive in cold and hostile regions because they generate their own body temperature. Yet we should bear in mind that these animals have undergone evolutionary changes to live under severe conditions. Quadrupeds, like llamas and wolves possess a thick fur and short limbs. This peculiarity affords them a better protection against the cold, for instance, the ear size of wild rabbits are much smaller than those from warmer regions. Large animals like pumas and deer which live in the uplands are bigger than those of the same species living in the tropical forests since it is well known that bigger animals can better keep their body warmth than small ones. Concerning birds, the biggest species of humming-birds inhabit the heights. They display amazing flapping movements that fluctuate between 50 and 80 flutters per second, they exhibit a marvelous dexterity when sucking nectar, catching insects or chasing away intruder humming-birds. They are usually found in metallic and iridescent colours. Due to their high metabolic system, they utilize a lot of energy, therefore, they are obliged to feed themselves constantly, otherwise they would soon perish. When the food is scarce, chiefly at night, they compensate this problem by reducing the rhythmic contractions of the heart from 1,200 beatings per minute to less than 100, and their body temperature from 38º C to about 14º C. In this way, humming-birds consume less energy.

Another superb bird of the heights is the andean condor. As opposed to the size of humming-birds, they are the largest and heaviest flying birds on earth. An adult specimen may weight around 25 pounds and their wingspan reaches up to 3 meters (9 feet). This windborne creature glides amazingly in the sky as if it were not making any effort, it feeds chiefly on carrion and seldom attacks small, unprotected animals. The condor has attracted the attention of reprobate hunters and merciless poachers, they kill them for the mere sake of killing and make futile ostentations of their hunting skills. This sordid and contemptible aggression against nature has led almost to the total extintion of condors.

Sparrow hawks and falcons are also dexterous flyers, they are much smaller than condors but they are capable of hovering, by this way, they observe minutely their prey, when they sight it, they abruptly plunge to catch it.

Some migratory species of birds reach the high moorlands while fleeing from the cold winter of the northern hemisphere. In this group we can quote the so-called snippers, and some aquatic birds. Among the indigens species of the uplands there are: "curiquinges" or carunculated caracaras, "guarros", "cuscungos" or owls. On the other hand, condors and gulls migrate short distances depending on the rainy season.

Wild horses roam through the large páramos of the National Park, they are indeed the remnants of the former huge estates around the mountain. Although they live and reproduce in a feral state, they all have an owner.

In general, The Cotopaxi National Park within its boundaries, represents a sanctuary for the aboriginal flora and fauna, thus some species have increased in number as in the case of the deer. Besides this, they have lost their natural fear to man. This peculiarity does not occur in other natural areas which are not protected, hence we may confidently assert that the flora and fauna are slowly disappearing due to excesive hunting, agricultural activities within natural areas and periodical Páramo fires.

With the exception of the Cotopaxi glaciers, the rocky cliffs of Rumiñahui and Morurco and the few scattered lakes, the rest of the Park territory comprises Páramo-grass. In Ecuador the word Páramo denotes the vegetation that grows from about 3,200 m to 4,800 m (10,500 to 15,750 feet) above sea level. It also connotes dry and swampy zones which are generally covered with the so-called Pajonal or Páramo-grass.

The south-western boundaries of the Park are the lowest and so are blessed with a favorable and benign climate with average temperatures of 10 º C and moderate winds. The slopes are festooned with flowers and *Stipa-ichu* (Páramo-grass) as well as small shrubs of the genus Diplostephium and Loricaria. Gorges provide good protection against the wind, for inside them the vegetation thrives better than on the open fields. Hence shrubs, orchids, reeds and dwarf trees are lush and abundant. In the altitude, near the glaciers, the gorges are not so deep and the vegetation disappears. On the open fields, the *Stipa-ichu* becomes smaller but a lot of flowers grow luxuriantly, thus dandelions, gentians, "ñachacs", arquitectas, chuquirahuas, "achupallas", lupins, and licopodium colonies constitute a high porcentage of the floral life. At higher altitudes plants develop shorter stalks and others are associated in compact colonies in order to protect themselves from the winds. All these plants have a very slow rate of development, for they may need a decade to gather enough energy to blossom.

Another well represented plant in the Páramo is the "Senecio". It grows within the moraines and sandy slopes. The leaves of this plant are characterized by their hairy nature and resistance to freezing temperatures; that is why they are commonly known as rabbit ears. In the moorlands and on the rocky walls of Yanasacha, just below the summit of Cotopaxi, there are species of lichens that live on bare rock. This form of life occurs at very high altitudes; in the case of Cotopaxi and Chimborazo we find them near 6,000 m (19,700 feet) and in the Himalaya mountain range close to 7,000 m (23,000 feet). In fact, lichens are compound, thallophytic plants, they are composed of a fungus in symbiotic union with an alga. The function of the fungus is to produce an acid that corrodes the rock, thus transforming the minerals into chemical substances that the alga absorbs. The fungus, due to its spongy nature collects a great deal of moisture whereas the alga uses photosynthesis and the aid of sunlight as a source of energy, transforming the carbon dioxide and the environmental humidity into nutrients.

The precarious existence of lichens at high altitudes depends much on the environmental conditions. There are years in which only a few days offer them the necessary warmth to grow. It may take half a century till the lichens cover a surface of 1 square cm, therefore, we may infer that a surface of 20 square cms might have needed centuries or perhaps millennia to come into being.

On the very top of snow-capped mountains, life does not exist at all. These cold and desolate spots are only reached by insects carried by the wind and occasionally by mountaineers desirous to satisfy their constant restlessness.

1. Chuquiragua, *Chuquiragua insignis.*
2. View of the volcano from the Limpiopungo lake.
3. Spring at the foot of Cotopaxi.
4. Marshland vegetation.
5. Stormy weather.
6. Dawn in the heights of Cotopaxi.
7. The crater,Cotopaxi.
8. Rabbit ears, *Senecio canescens.*
9. Lupins, *Lupinus sp.*
10. "Arquitecta",*Culcitium reflexum.*
11. *Werneria nubigena.*
12. Gentians, *Gentianella aff diffusa.*
13. "Lancetilla", *Castilleja pumilla.*
14. *Diplostephium sp.*
15. Licopodium, *Licopodium crassum.*
16. "Urcurosa", *Ranunculus guzmanii.*
17. "Popa", *Tristerix longebracteatus.*
18. Orchid, *Oncidium cucullatum.*
19. *Hypochaeris sessiliflora.*
20. Plumbeous finch, *Phrygilus unicolor.*
21. Bar-winged cinclodes, *Cinclodes fuscus.*
22. Noble snipe, *Gallinago nobilis.*
23. Andean gull, *Larus serranus.*
24. Sparrow hawk, *Falco sparverius.*
25. Andean lapwing, *Anas flavirostris.*
26. Andean hillstar, *Oreotrochilus stella.*
27. Andean condor, *Vultur gryphus.*
28. Black frog, *Atelopus ignescens.*
29. Carunculated caracara, *Phalcoboenus carunculatus.*
30. Andean wolf, *Duscycion culpaeus.*
31. Wild horses.
32. "Alpaca", *Lama pacos.*
33. Forest rabbit, *Sylvilagus brasiliensis.*
34. Virginian deer, *Odocoileus virginianus ustus.*
35. Cotopaxi volcano.
36. Andean teal, *Vanellus resplendens.*

3

4

5

6

8

9

10

11

13

14

15

16

18

19

20

21

22

23

25

26

27

28

31

32

35

36

NATIONAL PARK
GALAPAGOS

The Galápagos islands were formed by volcanic activity some million years ago when enormous eruptions rose up the land from the bosom of the ocean. At the beginning, the consecutive volcanic eruptions left eerie and desolate islands covered with blood-red lava fields and ash. Notwithstanding, this odd landscape was not as sterile as it looked, since the minerals expelled from the earth made them highly appropriated for the development of life. Plants were as a matter of course the first forms of life that colonised the islands. The first living creatures were conveyed from the mainland to the archipelago due to the constant buffeting of the winds. The former volcanic explosions that laid waste and upheaval to the islands started to cease with the exception of a few intermittent volcanoes and the fields turned green and fit for life.

A great deal of feathered creatures made this sanctuary their home; frigate birds, as well as several web-footed sea birds such as the albatros, sea gulls and boobies, discovered here a secure place to nest for they remained for centuries unmolested. Concerning small birds, the

Darwin finches are one of the most striking case of evolution to be quoted; these birds which originally came from the continent transported by the winds, provided Darwin with the vital clues to the question of evolution. He wrote his book on the origin of species after having concluded his long voyage around the world and his short stay in the Galápagos islands was of significant importance for that purpose.

The finches were continental birds and belonged to the same species, yet in the Galápagos they evolved into 13 different species. All of them show dissimilar traits and habits; one of them plucks for insects while another having a stronger beak does the same work of pecking birds. Another one which possesses an elongated beak sucks at flowers as if it were a humming-bird. There is another finch whose beak resembles that of a parrot and is specialised in cracking nuts and hard seeds. However, the most curious of all may be the one that uses a cactus spine to pick up larvae from the inside of the cactus trunks.

The very absence of predators contributed enormously to the variation of the species, as the case of the flightless cormorant which lost the ability to fly through time. Cormorants are heavy and voracious birds which like other birds require a lot of energy to lift themselves in the air, thus about 20% of the weight of flying birds is concentrated in the wing muscles. Yet, in the Galápagos cormorants' wings became small and futile, therefore unfit for flying. This change occurred due to the availability of an easy and abundant food supply, thus making flying unnecessary. Another interesting peculiarity of the islands is the presence of one antartic bird like the penguin and some species of sea gulls which are characteristic for their nocturnal-feeding-habits.

Another group of inhabitants that arrived to the islands from the mainland are reptiles, among them; marine and land iguanas, tortoises and lizards. The way that these animals arrived was presumably on top of treelogs which owing to the heavy floods during the rainy season in the coastal area, were carried to the ocean and consecuently by means of the Humboldt current to the Galápagos islands. Tortoises might have also arrived transported by the same current but probably not on top of treelogs. The tortoises are especially adapted to float in the ocean for weeks and without food, which in fact is enough to cover the 1,000 km (625 miles) that separate the islands from the continent.

Reptiles are quite fit for long ocean cruises, their skin is extremely waterproof and avoids dehydration caused by the salty water from the ocean. This was not the case of amphibians since they are not very resistant to salty water, hence their absence in the islands.

The Galápagos indigens mammals are mainly marine; sea lions, seals, porpoises and the so-called Orcas or killer whales are abundant around the islands. Concerning terrestrial mammals, they comprise two species of bats as well as two endemic species of rodents. Four species of native rodents have been already exterminated since man introduced the black rat which was a strong competitor.

The presence of man in the islands brought disastrous consequences to the ecological balance. Besides the black rat, other animals were introduced and let free in the fragile ecosystem of the archipelago, hence dogs, pigs and cats turned feral and became merciless predators preying on the defenseless endemic creatures. On the other hand, donkeys, cattle and feral goats destroyed the fragile vegetation.

This infelicitous chapter of the Galápagos islands started with the discovery of them by Fray Thomas de Berlanga in 1535. He was on a voyage from Panamá to Lima and his ship was suddenly swept westwards by the powerful Humboldt current and so the archipelago was accidentally discovered. As time elapsed, the Galápagos became well known for the tame creatures and especially for the giant tortoises that existed there. Consequently, many ships deviated their route to the islands to replenish their stores with fresh meat, for tortoises can resist months without food. These careless foreys corroborated to the almost total extintion of these amazing reptiles. Later on, pirates found in the Galápagos a perfect secluded place to hide themselves after their sea maurauding activities. Whalers and seal hunters arrived and depleted the giant tortoises and filled their vessels with costly seal furs.

Even now the ecological balance of the islands is in great peril. There are requests from powerful economic groups to obtain permits to navigate commercially around the islands. The number of visitors is increasing every year. The grim results that greed and ambition may provoke is a potential reality that in the future may come into full being and further endanger the balance of this unique paradise.

37. Sally light-foot crab, *Grapsus grapsus.*
38. Salty lake, Charles island.
39. Bartholomein island.
40. Sesuvium plants, south Plaza.
41. Charles island.
42. Sullivan bay, James island.
43. Suarez point, Hood island.
44. Sullivan bay, James island.
45. James island.
46. Bursera tree, *Bursera graveolens.*
47. Opuntia cactus, *Opuntia echtos.*
48. Highlands of Santa Cruz.
49. Vegetation on Barrington, *Cordia lutea.*
50. *Passiflora sp.*
51. Land iguana, *Conolophus subcristatus.*
52. Land iguana, *Conolophus subcristatus.*
53. Marine iguana, *Amblyrhynchus cristatus.*
54. Marine iguana, *Amblyrhynchus cristatus.*
55. Green-sea turtle, *Chelonia mydas.*
56. "El Junco" lake, Chatham island.
57. Charles island.
58. American oyster cartcher, *Haematopus palliatus.*
59. Giant tortoise, *Geochelone elephantopus.*
60. Sea lions, *Zalophus californianus.*
61. Sea lion, *Zalophus californianus.*
62. Yellow-crowned night heron, *Nyctanassa violacea.*
63. Lava heron, *Butorides sundevali.*
64. Magnificent frigate bird, *Fregata magnificens.*
65. Blue-footed booby, *Sula nebouxii.*
66. Masked booby, *Sula dactylatra.*
67. American flamingo, *Phoenicopterurs ruber.*
68. Red-billed tropic bird, *Phaeton aethereus.*
69. Swallow-tailed gull, *Nyctanassa violacea.*
70. Mockingbird from Hood island, *Nesomimus macdonaldi.*
71. Galapagos penguin, *Spheniscus mendiculus.*
72. Yellow warbler, *Dendroica petechia.*
73. Galapagos dove, *Zenaida galapagoensis.*
74. Male frigate bird, *Fregata magnificens.*
75. Fish school of "lisas", *Muguil sp.*

43

44

45

47

48

49

50

51

52

53

54

57

58

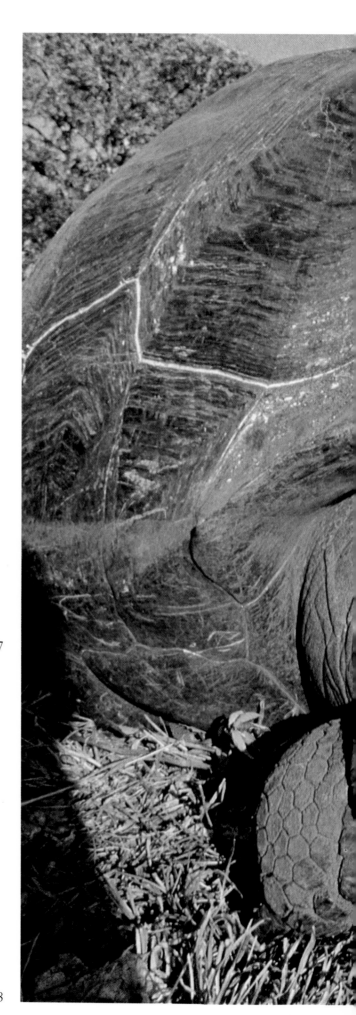

61

62

63

65

66

67

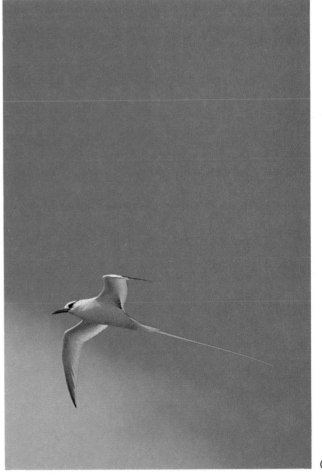

68

69

70

71

72

73

PODOCARPUS

The immense, vast geenery of the Amazon rain forest ends up in the highlands of the Andes, yet its undergrowth reaches an altitude of about 4,000 m (13,000 feet) above sea level. These dense jungle-clad hills are called sub-tropical or cloud forests. At this altitude, tropical trees are smaller than in the lowlands and some of the common species disappear, but others occur which characterize these high forests. At the boundaries with the high herbaceous Páramos, the forests are extremely foggy due to the high condensation rate. In these isolated uplands, where two dissimilar ecological systems meet, are some of the most biological riches.

Both National Parks; Sangay and Podocarpus are vastly clad with high cloud-forests, especially the latter has a very peculiar flora since it receives the climatic influence of the southern arid lowlands.

The huge massive Andes stops the wet clouds of the Amazon basin from reaching the inter-andean valleys, for they remain condensed in the eastern highland boundaries, thus causing constant mist and rain. All this is produced by the trade winds. Due to this weather, this region teems with a great variety of epiphytes such as orchids, mosses, lichens and bromeliads. These latter, like any other epiphyte grow nonparasitically upon the compost of mosses and lichens. They are chiefly found on tree branches and rock ledges in the mountain cliffs, they derive their nutrients from the air, water, dust etc, usually by means of their hanging vines. The leaves of bromeliaceous plants are in such a way made so that they collect rain water and form amazingly tiny ecological worlds. Some insects lay their eggs in the interior of these leaves, thus when the larvae come into life, they find enough supply of nourishment since a great variety of bacteria, protozoa and fungi dwell inside. Likewise, the larvae of insects and crustaceans represent the main food for spiders, toads and batrachians. In the lowlands, even crabs search for food in the bromeliaceous plants, while other animals look for them in order to quench their thirst.

There is maybe no other kind of flowers that draws so much the attention of man as the orchids, the great majority of them are epiphytes and therefore abundant in the primeval forests of Podocarpus. Many species of them are also found in the tropical lowlands.

The opinion that the orchid family has the most numerous species among plants that put forth flowers, is widely entertained by many botanists. Around 35,000 different species have been recorded. However, this calculation is rather approximate since in the tropical and cloud forests, new species are constantly being discovered. As opposed to the presumption that the majority of orchids are found in the tropical forests, it is indeed in the high-cloud forests where most species flourish. It is a remarkable fact, that in the cloud-forest exists much humidity and everlasting fog, which besides the strong winds represent a high advantage for the pollinization of these plants. Winds contribute to seed transport, and the inclination of the slopes permits sun rays to easily reach the ground, thus making a real habitat for orchids and other epiphytes. Much stress has been laid by some experimentalists on plants to produce hybrid and mongrel offsprings of orchids, thus rendering around 60,000 new species.

Orchids are reproduced through very tiny seeds which are well adapted to be wafted easily by the wind. They are produced in an indefinitely great number in a single plant. There are species that may contain 2 million seeds. In order to be fertilized, seeds ought to find certain fungi commonly known as *Mycorrhiza* from which they derive their principal nutrients to grow.

These plants are fertilised by means of pollinators such as nectar-feeding insects and birds. When an insect is allured by a flower, it rubs off some of the viscid matter and thus at the same time drags away some of the pollen grains. But not all the orchids yield nectar to attract insects and birds, about one third of them lacks nectar. To compensate this problem, they have acquired several variations through natural selection, namely, by means of mimicry. Some orchids imitate those that yield nectar while others produce agreable odors. The orchids pertaining to the *Onsidium* genus are usually fertilised by the male of the so-called Centris bee; the flower in this case displays the form of another male bee, supposedly a competitor which is normally attacked by the pugnacious males that consequently disperse the pollen grains after their vehement but frustrated assailment. Another species imitates the form of a female bee in order to attract the males. A very curious case is that of orchids yielding nauseating, and putrid odors to attract flies which are eminently liable for pollen dispersal. There is a peculiar co-relation of mutual benefit among some orchids and wasps, ants and other insects; orchids yield nectar which is the main nutriment for wasps and ants and these latter, at the same time keep orchids clear from some harmful orthopterous insects such as grasshoppers and crickets that chiefly feed on their petals and leaves.

The orchids of the *Cattleya* genus bear vivid and

attractive colours and are chiefly fertilised by humming-birds. These kind of orchids possess a tubular shape in whose interior is found the pollinium, so when the bird penetrates its beak, it rubs off much pollen which shall be consequently conveyed to the stigma of another flower. The high cloud-forest is considered a haven for silver-coloured humming-birds since they thrive on good fare. Insects and seeds also serve as nourishment for a great number of birds such as partridges and wild turkey.

76. Orchid, *Odontoglossum halii*.
77. Paramo grass with plants of the *Puya* genus.
78. High-cloud forest.
79. Paramo grass with plants of the *Tillandsia genus*.
80. Inside the cloud forest.
81. Trees of the cloud forest.
82. Sunset on the park.
83. Fern, *Cyathea Genus*.
84. Top of "Sabanilla" rank.
85. Orchid, *Cattleya máxima*.
86. Orchid, *Phragomiphedium besseae*.
87. Orchid, *Loricartia serra*.
88. Top of the rank with a *Werneria genus*
89. Fam.: *Orchidaceae*.
90. Orchid, *Epidendrum sp.*
91. Orchid, *Pleurothallis sp.*
92. Orchid, *Brassia logística*.
93. Orchid, *Epidendrum sp.*
94. Fam.: *Orchidaceae*.
95. Orchid, *Encyclia sp.*
96. Blue necked Tanager, *Tangara cyanicollis*.
97. *Gentianella cf. lehmannii*.
98. Anturtum, fam.: *Araceae*.
99. Orchid, *Góngora sp.*
100. Fam.: *Gesneriaceae*.
101. Urcurrosa, *Ranunculus guzmanii*.
102. Bromelia of flower, *Tillandsia sp.*
103. "Popa", *Tristerix longebracteatus*.
104. Anturtum leaf and "atuczara" flower
105. *Bomarea sp.*
106. Purple-throated sun angel, *Heliangelus viola*.
107. Chlorophnta pynnhophrys, young, *Chlorophonia pyrrhophrys*.
108. Bay-winged Hawk, *Parabuteo unicintus*.
109. Push-capped finch, *Catamblyrhinchus diadema*.
110. Baird´s Trogon, *Trogon viridis*.
111. Opossum, *Didelphis marsupialis*.
112. Least shrew, *Cryptotis montivaga*.

78

7

80

81

82

83

84

91

92

93

94

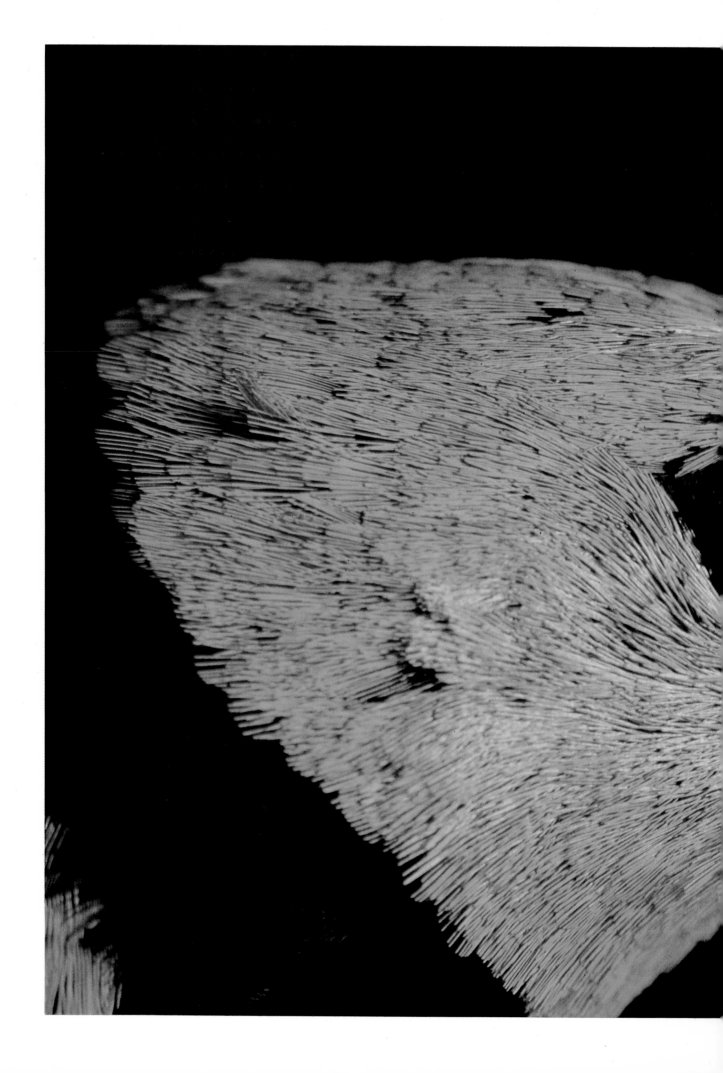

97

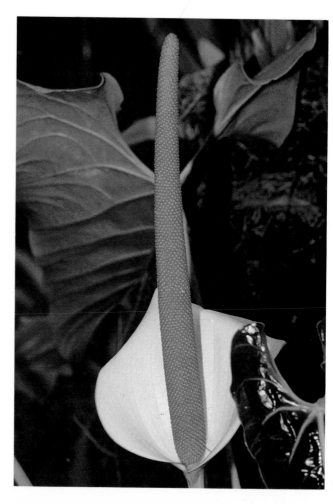

98

99

101

102

103

109

110

111

112

With the exception of lands protected by mangroves and estuaries, the majority of coastal land is being lost. Especially on the shores which are unprotected by beaches. The ocean`s forceful waves are continually eroding the rocky and compact clay cliffs. The crashing of the waves forms cornices and caves till the upper part of the cliff tumbles down into the ocean, therefore leaving protruding parts of hard rock or small islets. For a while, these islets and rocks will protect the cliffs from the waves, but eventually the scattered rocks will be also eroded, giving way to the ocean.

Amongst the rocks and shallow waters live a great deal of mollusks, shellfish, crabs and octopuses. Rocks, as opposed to sand, offer a solid ground which indeed is an ideal environment for the growth of marine algae. It is curious that marine plants do not possess the complexity of terrestrial ones, which have evolved in a different way in order to survive on earth. Marine plants, for instance, do not require any special mechanism to obtain water and nutrients, because the marine currents in which they live provide them with both water and nutrients and at the same time disperse their sexual cells. While some of these plants float on the water, others adhere themselves to the rocks. Their tubular roots are fit to adhere the plant to the rocks but by no means have an absorbent property. They can live out of the water only for a short while and are usually found just a bit above the lowest tide levels.

A relevant specimen of this zone is the so-called ghost crab that roams around the beaches in search of organic matter. Its eyes are on protruding stalks providing it with a vision of 360 º. It feeds itself with the help of its claws, thus grabbing small portions of sand which is then filtered in order to separate the organic matter contained there. Crabs possess hairy organs inside their mouth which serve them to separate all non-edible particles. The unnecessary matter is expelled, usually bearing the form of small sand balls which appear scattered on the beach.

Male crabs possess two dissimilar claws, the larger one is used to allure females while the small one serves as a means to feed themselves. They are chiefly known as fiddler crabs. Crabs, like many marine creatures breathe through gills, which are located inside their shells. Notwithstanding, these animals are able to spend long periods of time out of the water. There are also crabs which are strictly terrestrial. These crustaceans are provided with small chambers beside the gills, where the water is stored and the oxigen derived. Since the oxigen is consumed quickly, crabs make the water circulate through the mouth in order to enrich it with oxigen again.

The xerophytic forests which are located in the lower part of the Park have undergone various adaptations in the struggle for survival. As opposed to the cloud-forest where moisture and water are plentiful but sunlight is scarce, the xerophytic regions are quite the contrary. In these dry places there is a lot of sunlight but little water, therefore plants have developed different strategies to survive. A well known example is the struggle for territory. Some plants secrete venomous fluids through their roots in order to kill seeds that fall in the vicinity. Some trees gain territory by stretching their roots horizontally, thus preventing other seeds to germinate within their boundaries. In this way, these trees accumulate enough water supply in their marked territory. The characteristic plants of dry and desert regions are provided with spines which protect them from herbivorous animals.

These plants survive during drought periods by using two dissimilar strategies. For instance, the cactus plant gathers a great quantity of water during the rainy season which is supplied to the plant by means of its superficial roots, where it is consequenty stored in its tissues for future use. Due to the peculiarity of staying always green, these plants are called "suculent". The cactus leaves have a wide surface and are also provided with spines which protect them from dehidration and create a layer of cool air around them, thus insulating them from the parching heat and dryness. The cactus possesses chlorophyll in its stems and photosynthesis occurs without any loss of water. Its growth is very slow and may last several decades till the plant reaches adulthood.

The other survival strategy is called "estivation". For instance, acacia, guayacanes and kapok trees take advantage of the rainy season to grow, blossom and produce seeds. Yet, once the rains are over, they lose their leaves to avoid evaporation and remain in a torpid state until the next rainy season. Acacia trees put forth roots deep into the earth, reaching a considerable depth. These trees in the first stage of growth develop an intricate system of roots, up to 5 meters into the earth, some of them consequently gain access to underground water. The atentive observer will notice that in arid zones appears a tree that in relation to others maintains its green foliage all year round.

113. View toward south from Punta Los Frailes.
114. Kapok tree, *Ceiba trischistandra*.
115. Inside of a xerophytic forest during the rainy season.
116. Flower near the beach, *Commelina sp.*
117. Inflorescence during the rainy season, fam.: *Apocynaceae.*
118. Candelabrum cactus, *Armatocereus cartwrightianus*
119. *Opuntia* flower, in the background appears the Salango island.
120. Butterfly, *Marpesia sp.*
121. Red Acacia, *Senna incarnata.*
122. Moth larva, fam.: *Sphyngidae.*
123. Wild bee, *Euglossa sp.*
124. Cerambisido, *Callichroma sericium.*
125. Hermit crab, *Pagurus samuelis.*
126. Mouthless crab, fam.: *Paguridae.*
127. Fer de lance snake, *Equis bothrops.*
128. Cat-eyed snake, *Leptodeira septentrionalis ornata.*
129. Fer de lance devouring a small rodent.
130. Star snake, *Chironius carinatus flavopictus.*
131. Green iguana, *Iguana iguana iguana.*
132. Lan snail, land Gasteropod.
133. Horned frog, *Ceratophris stolzmanni scaphiopeza.*
134. Fulvous tree duck, *Dendrocygna* bicolor.
135. Laughing falcon, *Herpetotheres cachinnans.*
136. Long-tailed mocking-bird, *Mimus longicaudatus.*
137. Peruvian red-breasted meadow lark, *Stornella belicosa.*
138. Superciliated wren, *Thryothorus superciliaris.*
139. Snowy egret, *Egretta thula.*
140. Great egret, *Casmerodius albus.*
141. Spotted sand piper, *Actitis macularia.*
142. Burrowing owl, *Speotyto cunicularia.*
143. Black-crowned night-heron, *Nycticorax nycticorax.*
144. Sunset in the Frailes beach.
145. Opposum, *Virula sp.*
146. Archeological pieces of the zone, collection Cruz de Perón.
147. Brown pelican, *Pelecanus occidentalis.*
148. Aerial view of the Machalilla village.

115

11

117

118

121

122

123

124

125

126

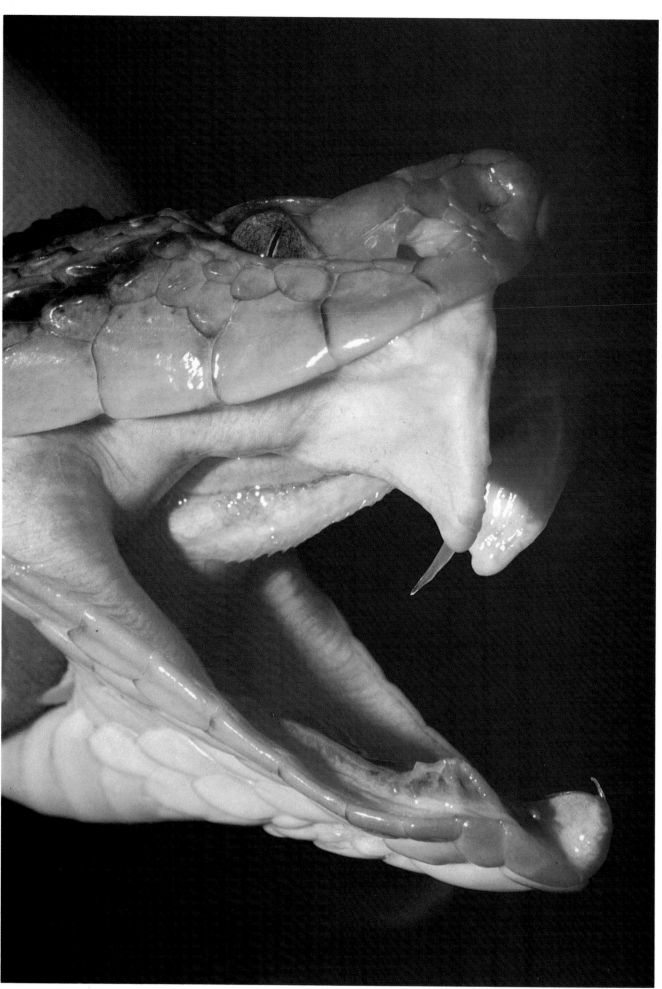

128

129

130

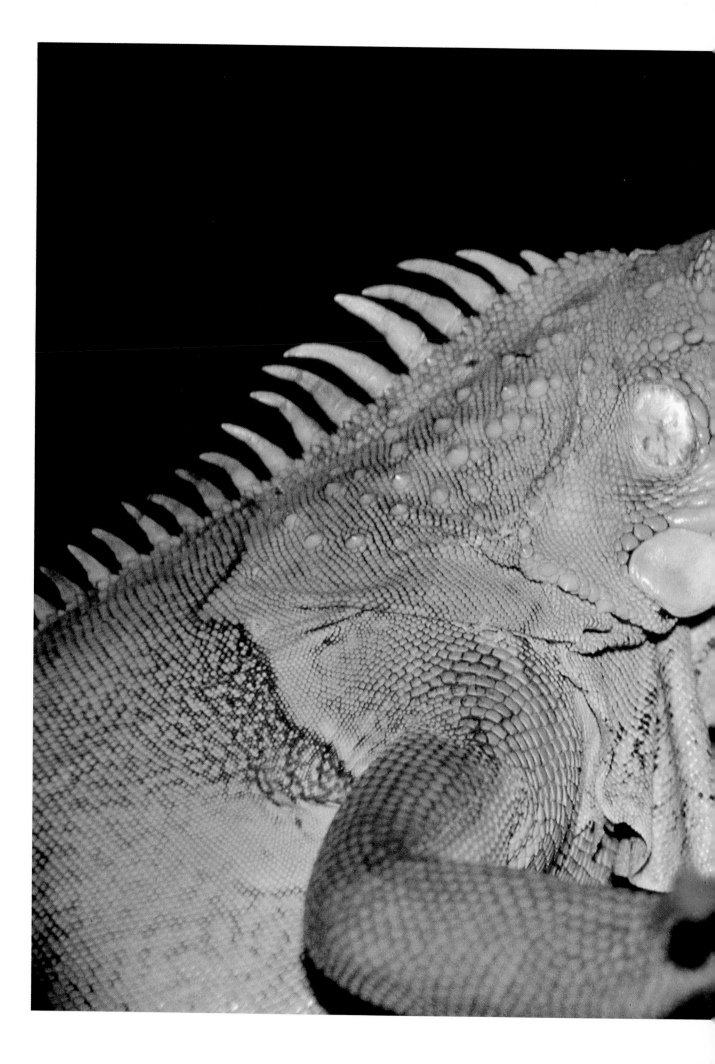

135

136

137

138

139

140

141

142

143

144

145

147

148

NATIONAL PARK

SANGAY

The tropical rain forest affords shelter to an abundant variety of insects, arachnids and centipedes as well as other tiny creatures, which in fact represent the main source of food to a great number of birds, amphibians, reptiles, fishes and even to certain predatory insects and plants. This is indeed, an example that corroborates the theory of natural selection. Invertebrates display amazing adaptations to the life in the jungle, for their camouflage in the underbrush is admirable. There are leaf insects whose wings resemble certain kinds of leaves with their corresponding colour and shape. Even the fungi which usually grow on the leaves appear depicted on the wings with remarkable perfection. There are insects that imitate twigs thus making them undistinguishable from the surrounding environment, like the case of stick insects which at the menacing presence of enemies camouflage themselves in the branches of trees in order to protect themselves.

If we devote our time to observe this intriguing tiny world, we shall be surprised at seeing thorns suddenly move away, twigs and bird droppings drag hurriedly along when we approach them as well as flowers flutter their petals tremulously and fly away when we try to pick them up.

The process of mimicry has been affected through natural selection, and a remarkable example is that of butterflies, for they imitate poisonous species as means of concealment and protection. Some imitate, for instance, the colours of the least palatable kinds which are invariably rejected by birds and other predators. Certain species of butterflies have acquired a marvelously deceitful appearance by displaying designs of big eyes on their wings, in order to be mistaken for bigger animals. By this way, they avoid being devoured by enemies. Another species of butterflies has quite translucent wings which make them appear as if they were invisible. There are harmless flies which mimic aggresive wasps.

Mimicry is not only used by species searching concealment but also by predators. This is the case of innumerable spiders that have acquired the surrounding colours to hide themselves. For instance, one of various predaceous insects is the praying Mantis which imitates the colour of moss as well as that of twigs and leaves.

Concerning reptiles, similar cases of mimicry also occur, like several species of harmless snakes which are tarned with the skins of dreadful corals in order to protect themselves from their enemies. On the other hand, real venomous snakes as well as other animals may be undergoing considerable variations to differ themselves in colour from their imitators.

Lizards are liable to change the appearance of their skin according to circumstances, thus acquiring the colours of the environment in which they are. For instance they can conceal themselves by using darkish, greenish and yellowish hues.

Mammals also display patterns of mimicry; the spotted jaguar for instance, has a skin which makes it indistinguishable in the underbrush. However, ironically due to this natural endowment, it is a common prey of unscrupulous hunters and mere murdering poachers which are cutting down the population of jaguars and consequently tipping the ecological balance toward failure. Men have come to apply greed and vanity against what bountiful fate had wrought. Other mammals are likewise risking extintion, the tapir and the spectacled bear are deem to meet their doom one day. One remarkable example which undoubtedly has undergone different variations in the struggle for life is the sloth, since it lumbers so slowly, thus making it ubiquitous, especially on top of trees where it usually dwells.

The spectacled bear is an inhabitant of sub-tropical forests and it is the only specimen of its genus in entire Latin-America and the southern hemisphere. Its name is due to the white eye patches which make it unmistak-

able, each individual has its own particular traits and it is very difficult to find two similar specimens.

Some birds are furnished with conspicuously bright colours, especially in the tropical and high cloud forests. Not only toucans, macaws, parrots and cocks of the rock display ostentatious colours, but also carrion-eating scavengers such as the king vulture. As opposed to its dull-coloured immediate congeners, it has a gaudy plumage.

As a matter of fact, we explore the jungle in order to sight large animals, but if we were to devote our patience to observe tiny life forms, then we shall be enraptured by the delights that this world may afford.

Sangay is perhaps the most inscrutable volcano, to catch a glimpse of it is quite difficult since it lies on the eastern Cordillera and is constantly overcast. The approach to the base camp starts in the inter-andean valleys and takes a march of three days. If luck accompanies the observer and the day is clear, the spectacle goes well beyond the stuff of dreams; amazing eruptions occur with intervals of 10 and 25 minutes, some produce overwhelming clatter while others are silent. During the clear, starry nights, flying red rocks and glowing lava expelled from the bosom of the crater can be easily observed, the whole awe-inspiring spectacle resembles a huge festival of fireworks.

The ascent to the summit is not always possible to accomplish, it depends much on the conditions of the volcano. Notwithstanding, if it allows the climber to reach the top, then the scenery is spell binding and the explosions superb.

Not far away toward the north, lies the extinct volcano "Altar". Its eroded crater bears the form of a horseshoe with its wide opening facing west. The whole mountain is covered with big glaciers with the exception of the vertical rock walls whose ascents are technical and comprise serious undertaking and risk.

Farther to the north looms the Tungurahua volcano, despite its dormant condition it is still active. The normal approach to the top is fairly easy and gorgeous. Two days are required to accomplish this climb and its route comes across subtropical rain forests, snow fields, and the smoking crater.

152

153

154

158

159

160

161

162

163

164

165

166

167

168

170

171

172

175

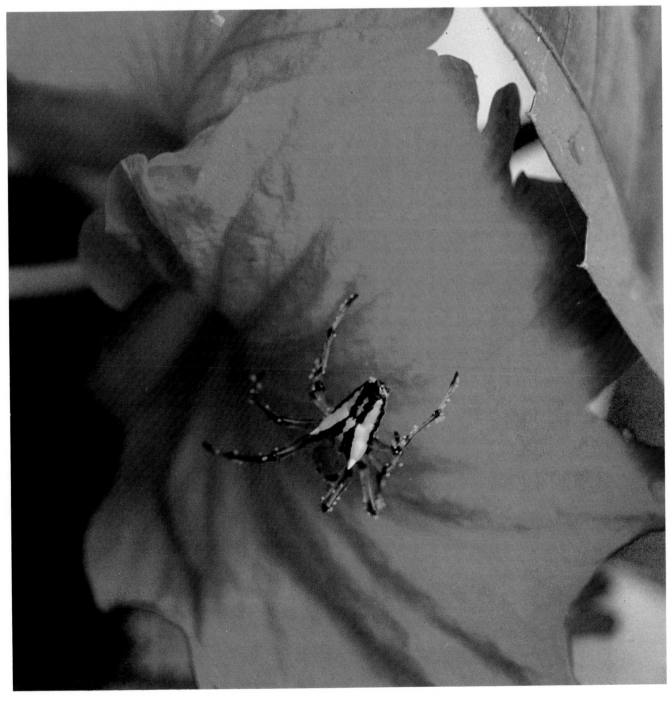

176

177

178

180

181

182

184

186

187

NATIONAL PARK

YASUNI

Nowhere else on earth is there so much concentration of sunlight, moisture due to the condensation of the atmosphere and heat as in the Amazon rain forests. All these extremely favorable environmental conditions which make life suitable, have somehow remained unaltered through the millennia since the last glacial period. The yearly changes in the jungle are minimal, thus the amount of sunlight and the average temperatures are fairly uniform. In the rain forests there exists only a rainy seasonal difference which consists in a spell of normal precipitation and another of heavy downpours and floods. In this amazingly stable environment, the evolution process has perfectly worked out yielding enormous diversities of species that occupy the utmost ecological niches.

Some entomologists maintain that in a single hectare of Amazon jungle exist more than 40,000 different species of insects, arachnids, mites and centipedes, and in the same area, there are more than 100 species of huge trees, almost more species than in North America and Europe together. For the common visitor this astonishing diversity is not evident since all the trees and leaves look alike. The difference between trees can be only perceived when they blossom. Notwithstanding, the blossom occurs on the very tree tops thus making it difficult to recognize the flowers.

The above mentioned climatic conditions determine that trees blossom at different times, some do every 6 months while others do in quite irregular periods hence apparently displaying ilogical processes, for instance: there are inflorescence periods that may last up to 10 years. Anyway, this natural process functions astonishingly since trees of the same species blossom at the same time in vast extensions of the jungle.

Some seeds of the big trees are provided with hairs and so are suited to fly considerable distances, for they are easily wafted by the wind. The heavier seeds are in the core of succulent fruits that allure toucans and monkeys, consequently scattering the seeds on other places. The so-called winged seeds possess small wings that allow them to fly, other seeds are admirably adapted for transport by pollinators.

The canopy of leaves and branches is so thick that only 3% of the sunlight reaches the soil, therefore, it is very difficult for the new seeds to obtain the necessary energy to develop. Those that germinate and receive little or no light, remain for decades of the size of small shrubs. When a big tree falls down whether for old age or due to a heavy downpour, there is consequently an open space that permits sunlight to penetrate into the thicket allowing new seeds and young trees to grow. This advantage is also taken by the seeds of plants that usually grow by the river beds or near lakes, for instance, the so-called Cecropias and Heliconias due to the miracle of sunlight develop green and wide leaves. As a matter of fact, there is for a while an open space in the jungle, but eventually the fast-growing underbrush will cover again the light tunnel.

Some plants have developed different strategies to compensate the lack of sunlight. For instance, the seeds of certain species of trees and especially those from the Ficus family are prone to germinate on top of the compost of decaying lichens and mosses which are normally located on the tree branches. The young Ficus starts stretching down its aerial roots in order to find nutrients and water in the air. Notwithstanding, as time passes by the aerial roots become thick and strong thus wrapping themselves around the tree. Besides this, the Ficus develops a lot of leaves in the upper part of the tree, thus producing shadow upon it. All these inconveniences cause the death of the tree, whereupon, the Ficus has developed stronger roots and can stand independently.

Hence, considering the exuberance of the jungle, we may perhaps infer that its soil should be extremely fertile, but indeed its organic layer is relatively thin and poor. What therefore keeps the rain forest alive and provides it with the essential nutrients is the decomposition of vegetable and organic matter. While in the forests of North America and Europe, any vegetable matter requires at least 7 years to decompose, in the Amazon basin it needs 4 or 5 weeks to vanish completely. Hence this soil is not thoroughly appropriate for agriculture, thus once the jungle has been cleared, the thin humus layer will be wiped off with the frequent rains.

During the last glacial periods, the world had quite a different geological shape. Some 10,000 years ago, when the last glacial period took place, the polar ice covered the north of France and joined it with the British isles. The sea level around the world was assuredly 10 m lower than today.

In South America the glaciers descended to an altitude of about 3,000 m (9,800 feet) above sea level. As a result, they left behind enormous traces, such as wide and elongated depressions which at the present day are inhabited and cultivated valleys.

The former subtropical jungle of the Amazon basin was transformed into a huge herbaceous plain, notwithstanding, some remnants of rain forest were preserved. These sanctuaries were therefore the habitat of innumerable species. Once the glacial periods were over, these jungle islands began to spread over the big savannah giving shelter to more species than the rest of the jungle. One of these sanctuaries existed along the Napo river basin where nowadays the Yasuni National Park is located.

In the tropical forests there is a great quantity of fruits, seeds, leaves and roots which constitute the nourishment of innumerable insects. A very curious case is that of the Leaf cutting ant; these tiny creatures have developed a complicated process to transform vegetable matter into edible fare. Hundreds of them can be sighted collecting certain kind of leaves which are then carried to their nests to be thoroughly processed. The leaves are first cut and chewed, then stored and fermented, whence a special kind of fungus appears upon this dead organic matter which in fact is the food that sustains their lives. It is admirably strange that other kinds of fungi are not capable to subsist upon the organic matter assembled by the ants.

The tropical forest is indeed the most appropriated world for amphibians and batrachians, and they thrive in amazingly varied forms. There are frogs of huge size such as the *Xeratophris* which feeds chiefly on small vertebrates. In order to catch his prey, the *Xeratophris* hides himself in the underbrush and awaits there till a small creature passes by. As opposed to this frog, there are very small ones, the *Dendrobates* which is a genus of the most conspicuously coloured frogs. Their colours serve them as a means of protection against predators since they reveal that it is highly venomous, it is indeed one of the most poisonous creatures on earth, thus more venomous than the fiercest viper. The poisonous fluid passes through the skin of the predator by osmosis..

Some other species of *dendrobates* may be only venomous when their skin comes into close contact with an open wound or when devoured by larger predators.

Another striking case is that of the *Centrolenella resplendens*. This is a small toad commonly known as the glass toad due to the high degree of transparency of his skin that allows to see its bones and beating heart. Most of these frogs and toads have adapted themselves perfectly to live in the jungle. They have developed special limbs to climb trees and branches and to adhere themselves to the leaves. Since the great majority of batrachians live in a damp or aquatic habitat, these jungle frogs find enough humidity of the rain forest carring an independent life from the water.

The jungle is also the habitat of reptiles; among them turtles, lizards and snakes. The mythical huge snakes which are lurking in the underbrush waiting to jump on a passing tapir or man do not exist. The biggest of them all are the aquatic anaconda and the terrestrial boa. On the other hand, the majority of jungle snakes are thin and small.

Concerning mammals, they have also demonstrated exceptional adaptations to the jungle life. It is a remarkable fact, that south american primates poseess a fifth limb, namely the prehensile tail. Monkeys in Asia and Africa do not have such a tail. The same kind of tail is found in various quadrupeds; for instance, the so-called cusumbo, some marsupials such as opossums and one species of ant bear.

Among other inhabitants of the rain forest which are worth mentioning, we have the tapir and deer, as well as the big herbivorous quadrupeds like the "Guantas" and "Guatusas". Concerning rodents, there are a lot of mice, shrew mice and the biggest rodent in the world, namely the "Capibara" which usually dwells by the river beds. In regard to predators, we find still in great numbers; jaguars, ocelots and pumas.

189. Boa constrictor, *Boa c. constrictor.*
190. Huge trees in the jungle.
191. Palm- tree flower.
192. Heliconia flower, *Heliconia aff. longa.*
193. Vegetation in the jungle floor, *Calathea viechii.*
194. *Centropogom iagiata.*
195. Aerial view of the jungle.
196. Forest destruction caused by oil companies.
197. Fam.: *Solanaceae.*
198. Heliconia flower, *Heliconia sp.*
199. Lady bee on a mushroom.
200. Stick insect, fam.: *Phasmidae.*
201. Leave-cutting ants, *Atta laevigata afe.*
202. Stick insects copulating.
203. Spider getting ready to devoure its victim, *Nephila claviceps.*
204. Spiny spider, *Micrathena sp.*
205. Moth, Lepidopter.
206. Molting orthopteron.
207. Courious kind of grasshopper, fam.: *Tetigonidae.*
208. Butterfly, fam.: *Brassolidae.*
209. Butterfly on top of a mushroom, *Tithorea harmania.*
210. 88 butterfly, *Catagrama sp.*
211. Butterfly, *Eurytides harmodius afe.*
212. Snake, *Lepthophis aethula nigromargi.*
213. Tree-dwelling frog, *Hyla boans.*
214. Leave frog, *Hemyphractus proboscideus.*
215. Poison-arrow frog, fam.: *Dendrobatidae.*
216. Glass frog, *Centrollenela resplendens.*
217. Poison-arrow frog, *Dendrobates parvulus.*
218. Horned frog, *Ceratophrys cornuta.*
219. Tree-dwelling frog, *Phyllomedusa tomopterna.*
220. Tree-dwelling snake, *Imantodes c. cenchoa.*
221. Garden's boa, *Corallus e. enydris.*
222. "Cordoncillo", *Oxybelis argenteus.*
223. Gecko, *Gonatodes sp.*
224. Lizard, *Mabuya mabouya.*
225. Black caiman devouring a frog, *Paleosuchus trigonatus.*
226. Lizard, *Polychrus marmoratus.*
227. Ocelot, *Felis pardalis.*
228. Squirrel monkey, *Saimiri sciureus.*
229. Dragon fly, orden: *Odonata.*

190

191

192

193

194

195

196

197

198

200

201

203

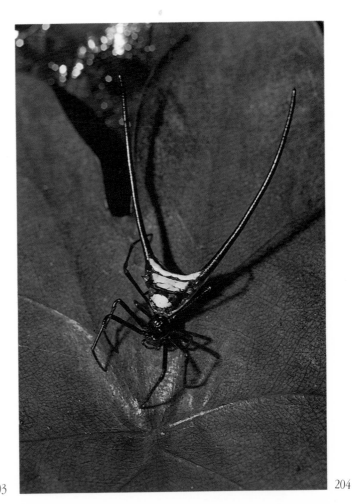

204

205

213

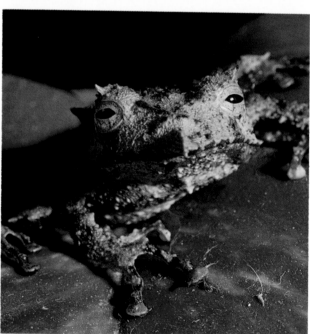

214

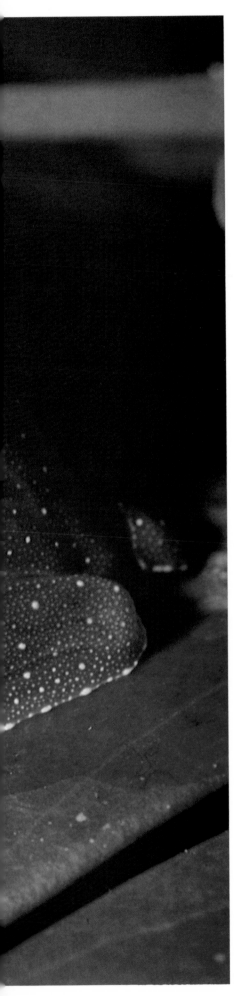

216

217

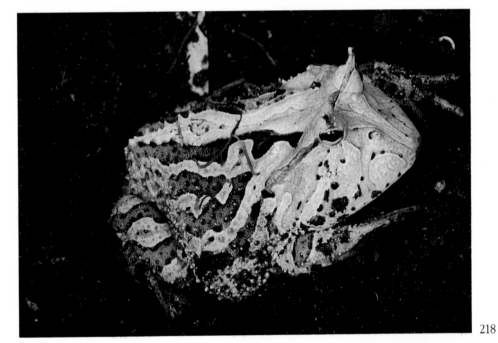

218

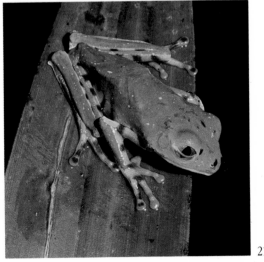

219

220

221

222

223

225

226